AMAZING INVENTORS & INNOVATORS

SAMUEL MORSE

LYNN DAVIS

Consulting Editor, Diane Craig, M.A./Reading Specialist

Super Sandcastle

An Imprint of Abdo Publishing
abdopublishing.com

abdopublishing.com

Published by Abdo Publishing, a division of ABDO, PO Box 398166, Minneapolis, Minnesota 55439. Copyright © 2016 by Abdo Consulting Group, Inc. International copyrights reserved in all countries. No part of this book may be reproduced in any form without written permission from the publisher. Super SandCastle™ is a trademark and logo of Abdo Publishing.

Printed in the United States of America, North Mankato, Minnesota
062015
092015

Editor: Liz Salzmann
Content Developer: Nancy Tuminelly
Cover and Interior Design and Production: Mighty Media, Inc.
Photo Credits: Library of Congress, Shutterstock, Wikicommons

Library of Congress Cataloging-in-Publication Data

Davis, Lynn, 1981- author.
Samuel Morse / Lynn Davis ; consulting editor, Diane Craig, M.A./Reading Specialist.
    pages cm. -- (Amazing inventors & innovators)

Audience: K to grade 4

ISBN 978-1-62403-725-2

1. Morse, Samuel Finley Breese, 1791-1872--Juvenile literature. 2. Inventors--United States--Biography--Juvenile literature. 3. Artists--United States--Biography--Juvenile literature. 4. Telegraph--Juvenile literature. 5. Morse code-- Juvenile literature. I. Title.

TK5243.M7D38 2016
621.383'092--dc23
[B]
                    2014046601

Super SandCastle™ books are created by a team of professional educators, reading specialists, and content developers around five essential components—phonemic awareness, phonics, vocabulary, text comprehension, and fluency—to assist young readers as they develop reading skills and strategies and increase their general knowledge. All books are written, reviewed, and leveled for guided reading, early reading intervention, and Accelerated Reader™ programs for use in shared, guided, and independent reading and writing activities to support a balanced approach to literacy instruction.

CONTENTS

SAMUEL MORSE

Samuel Morse was an American **innovator**. He didn't invent the telegraph. But he knew he could make it better. He also helped invent Morse code.

Morse telegraph key

Morse telegraph receiver

SAMUEL MORSE

BORN: April 27, 1791, Charlestown, Massachusetts

FIRST MARRIAGE: Lucretia Pickering Walker, September 29, 1818, Concord, New Hampshire. They had three children, Susan, Charles, and James. She died in 1825.

SECOND MARRIAGE: Sarah Elizabeth Griswold, August 10, 1848, Utica, New York. They had four children, Samuel, Cornelia, William, and Edward.

DIED: April 2, 1872, New York, New York

PRESIDENTIAL PAINTER

Morse's first job was as a painter. He painted pictures of people.

Samuel Morse self-portrait

He even painted two United States presidents!

Morse's portrait of John Adams, second president of the United States

Morse's portrait of James Monroe, fifth president of the United States

LOST LOVE

Morse was out of town. He was working on a painting. He got a letter. His wife was sick. He raced home to be with her.

Morse's portrait of the Marquis de Lafayette

She died before he got there. He received the letter too late. Morse was very sad. He wanted to be able to send messages faster.

Morse's portraits of his first wife, Lucretia, and their children

ELECTRIC MESSAGES

Morse met
Charles Thomas
Jackson. Jackson
experimented
with electricity
and magnets.

Charles
Thomas
Jackson

Jackson's experiments gave Morse an idea.
He saw a way to make the telegraph better.

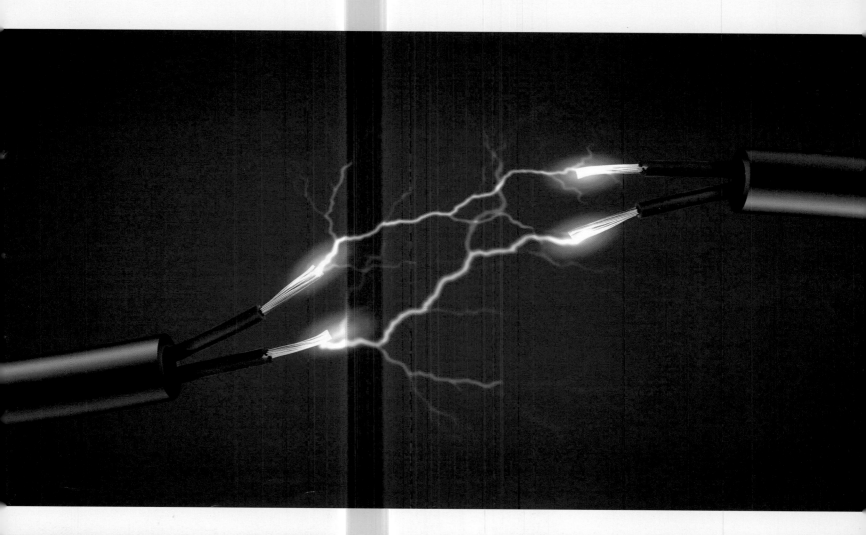

OUT OF MANY, ONE

Other telegraphs used a lot of wires. Each letter had its own wire. Morse wanted to use just one wire.

Samuel Morse, 1840

Leonard Gale

Leonard Gale was a scientist. He helped Morse with his telegraph.

Cooke & Wheatstone telegraph, 1837

ANOTHER TELEGRAPH

Most places used Morse's telegraph. But the United Kingdom used a different one. Two Englishmen made it. Their telegraph had many wires.

RELAY RACE

The first messages couldn't go far. Then Morse added relays. They were spaced out along the wire.

RELAY MAGNET.

A message went from the telegraph to the first relay. The relay sent the message to the next relay. It could be **repeated** for miles!

READING BETWEEN THE LINES

The message came out as a line on paper. The line went up and down.

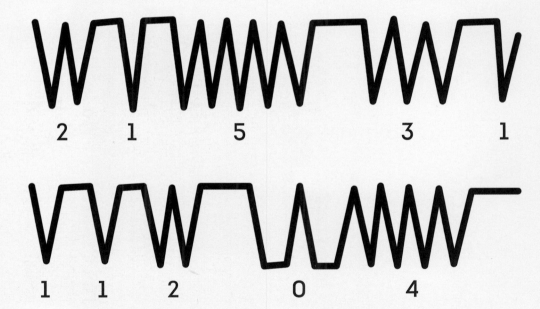

Example of an early telegraph message

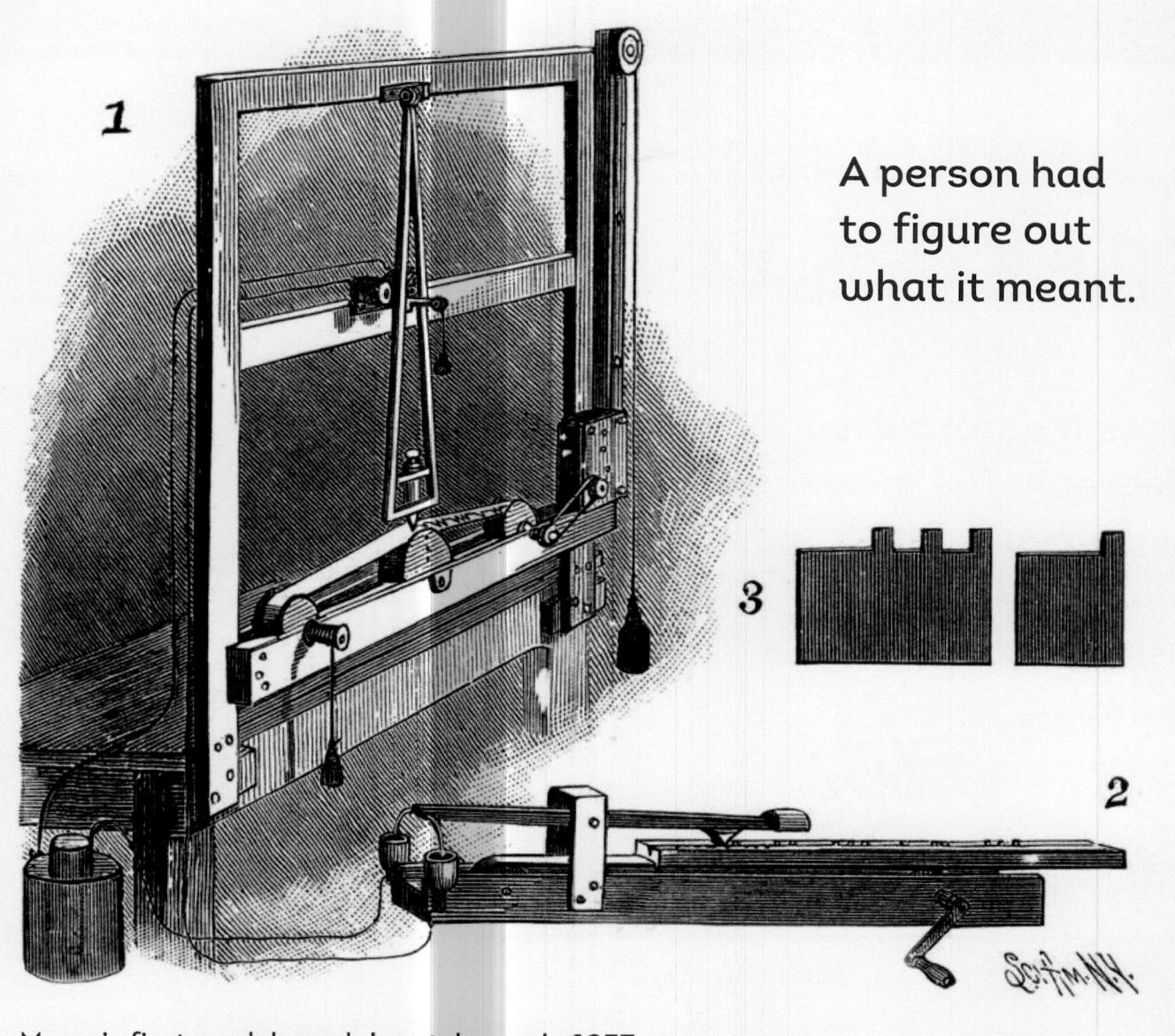

A person had to figure out what it meant.

Morse's first model pendulum telegraph, 1837
1. Recording Receiver 2. Port-rule 3. Type

A BETTER TELEGRAPH

Morse made another telegraph. The messages used a new code. It was made up of dots and **dashes**. It was easy to figure out.

First long-distance telegraph message, May 24, 1844

This sentence was written from Washington by me at the Baltimore Terminus at 8ʰ 45 min. A.M. on Friday May 24ᵗʰ 1844, being the first ever transmitted from

W   h   a   t   h   a   t   h   G